S0-AVO-430

# MASTERMIND DINNERS

*by*

## JAYSON GAIGNARD

VERSION 1.0

TO STAY UP TO DATE WITH NEW VERSIONS,
AND GET ACCESS TO FREE BOOK RESOURCES,
VISIT MASTERMINDDINNERS.COM

MANUSCRIPT FORMATTED BY: ERIN TYLER
ISBN: 9780692360026

# As a Thank You

FOR INVESTING IN THIS
BOOK, I'D LIKE TO GIVE
YOU THE AUDIOBOOK
VERSION FOR FREE!

Visit *MastermindDinners.com* to take
*advantage of this exclusive offer.*

"JAYSON IS A SUPER-CONNECTOR. He is two degrees of separation from everyone you want to meet. His Mastermind Dinners are the only invitations I accept because I know each one will change my life."

- JAMES ALTUCHER,
WSJ BEST-SELLING AUTHOR OF *CHOOSE YOURSELF*

"JAYSON'S DINNERS ARE FANTASTIC--I'm thrilled he's sharing his secrets with the rest of the world."

- A.J. JACOBS,
MULTIPLE *NEW YORK TIMES* BEST-SELLING AUTHOR

"DINNERS MAY BE THE MOST POWERFUL way to build deep, authentic relationships quickly. And Jayson is the master at organizing them. You will walk away with many game-changing ideas to transform the impact of your dinners."

- MICHAEL SIMMONS,
FOUNDER OF IEMPACT.ORG AND CONTRIBUTOR AT *FORBES*

"EVERY TIME I CONNECT WITH JAYSON (even through email!) something amazing shakes out of it. He's like a magnet for amazing talent and good people."

- JORDAN HARBINGER,
FOUNDER OF *THE ART OF CHARM*

"IF YOU WANT TO FORM LIFELONG relationships with like minded positive individuals then consume everything Jayson says and does. He walks the talk and is the perfect person to guide anyone in forming lifelong relationships with the top people on the planet."

- DR. JEREMY WEISZ,
FOUNDER OF INSPIREDINSIDER.COM

"THE WORLD IS FULL OF PEOPLE who claim to network and add value. Jayson puts them all on notice by being one of the most genuine and grateful souls out there. I'm very excited to jump into his brain and steal his tips for hosting remarkable group events."

- BRENT SUMMERS,
ENTERPRISE MANAGER AT CONTACTUALLY

"JAYSON HAS CREATED a step-by-step guide that gives you a repeatable formula you can use to host your own Mastermind Dinners, no matter what industry you are in, to grow your impact, influence and income. He's one of the most well connected people I know and it's not because of luck or chance. It's because of this formula. Follow what he says and use it and you will see huge results."

- JOHN CORCORAN,
FORMER CLINTON WHITE HOUSE WRITER; ATTORNEY & ADVISOR TO ENTREPRENEURS

"IF YOU'VE EVER WANTED TO LEARN how to connect more authentically with people 'out of your league' and have a blast while doing it, buy this book! Jayson practices what he preaches and it's great to see him sharing his wisdom here."

- UJ RAMDAS,
CO-AUTHOR OF *THE FIVE MINUTE JOURNAL*

"WHEN IT COMES TO BUILDING meaningful relationships, Jayson is a true master. His ability to gather fascinating people from around the world and connect them in ways that spark new friendships, profitable business deals, and life-long connections is without parallel. If you want to apply his techniques and develop this crucial skill for yourself, reading Mastermind Dinners is a MUST!"

- JOEY COLEMAN,
CHIEF EXPERIENCE COMPOSER AT FIRST 100 DAYS

"JAYSON'S DINNERS ALWAYS create 10x more value for my life and business then the time they take to attend. He's a master curator."

- DAN MARTELL,

AWARD-WINNING ANGEL INVESTOR & FOUNDER OF CLARITY.FM

"HONESTLY, I'M A BIT FRUSTRATED Jayson is releasing this book. His approach to networking is so effective, that I wish he would just keep it a secret. However, having been the guest at one of his amazing Mastermind Dinners, I was blown away by what a thoughtful, effective, value driven strategy he was using to build and delight his network. Since he is releasing his secrets to the world, I highly, highly suggest you pick up this book and take advantage of the brilliance within."

- JASON CONNELL,

FOUNDER OF IGNITEDLEADERSHIP.COM

"JAYSON IS A GREAT EXAMPLE of a guy who went from being socially awkward and "normal" to being a superconductor and business magnate. This isn't exaggeration, it's exactly what he did. The question is, 'How?' "Mastermind Dinners," shows you how. In this book you won't find tricks, tactical advice, or manipulative techniques for getting a quick "yes." If all you want is a quick yes, go buy some other garbage networking book... God knows there's plenty out there. Mastermind Dinners is different - it lays out a strategic plan for building long term relationships that are both professional and personal--relationships that will be there, not just during the good times, but the bad times too."

- ISAIAH HANKEL, PH.D,

BEST-SELLING AUTHOR AND INTERNATIONAL SPEAKER

"JAYSON UNDERSTANDS NOT JUST THE POWER of getting the right people in a room to "break bread," but also how to maximize the impact each person gives and receives during their time together. His mastery of relationship building, his humility, and his desire to serve those in his network is second to none. This book is an outpouring of his continuous desire to add value to the game changers he surrounds himself with and any leader would be wise to dive into this wisdom immediately."

- JOHN RUHLIN,
FOUNDER OF THE RUHLIN GROUP

"WHEN I FIRST MET JAYSON he asked me what I wanted to get out of his event. My response was simple: "I just want to meet people like me." In the two years that followed, my business has grown many times over and I credit Jayson's super-connector skills for much of that growth.

- JONATHAN GOODMAN,
FOUNDER OF THEPTDC.COM

"EVERY DETAIL MATTERS while planning a world-class unique experience—and Jayson certainly covers all of them in this excellent book.

- DEREK COBURN
BEST SELLING AUTHOR OF NETWORKING IS NOT WORKING

# TABLE OF CONTENTS

"SHOW ME YOUR FRIENDS, AND I'LL SHOW YOU YOUR FUTURE…"

~JOHN WOODEN

# PREFACE

*"There are three types of people in the world… those who make things happen, those who watch things happen, and those who wonder what happened."*

T he mere fact that you've picked up this book is a good indication that you're the type of person that takes action. And life rewards those who take action.

I believe that good judgment often comes from experience, and experience often comes from bad judgment. My hope is that by being transparent about my journey, you can leverage my successes, and avoid my mistakes.

The catalyst that has brought me the majority of my success over the past two years comes from hosting something I like to call 'Mastermind Dinners.' These dinners have taken me from being bankrupt on virtually every level of my life to personal and professional heights which include launching a #1 rated business podcast, spending a week with three-time best-selling author Tim Ferriss in Argentina, meeting up with skate legend Tony Hawk at his offices in California to sit in on his radio show, and now running one of the world's most exclusive events for entrepreneurs.

The speed by which I've turned my life around can easily be replicated and I've created this book to show you how. The key is the way in which you create and cultivate your relationships, and the concept of Mastermind Dinners is your vehicle.

# NO PRESSURE,
# NO DIAMONDS

*When you hit rock bottom in life, you'll be left with two things: the integrity of your word, and your relationships. Never tarnish your word, and always invest in your relationships.*

For years I was what most would consider 'successful.' In my early twenties I could do virtually anything I wanted. I had the freedom of both time and money. But even with this abundance of money and free time, something was still missing. I found myself trying to answer some really tough questions like "Why am I here?" "Will I be remembered?" and "How many people will show up to my funeral?" and was forced to admit I wasn't happy with the answers I was giving myself. My purpose was clouded and I knew that if I died tomorrow I wouldn't leave much worth remembering behind.

Coincidentally it was around this same time when I realized that business was going exceedingly well. I was earning 22 times the national average income, but I wasn't 22 times happier than the average male and certainly not 22 times healthier. In fact, two years prior (at the age of 23), I had kidney complications because of stress. What others may have seen as reason to celebrate left me jaded.

It became clear to me that money and happiness scale very differently.

It also became glaringly obvious that I had never taken the opportunity to stop and question things... but it was too late. I knew I had built the wrong business, which had led me to attract the wrong customers.

I made money to buy things and then worried about the things once I bought them. Because of this I lived in a constant state of anxiety.

On the outside I was leading a multi-million dollar e-commerce company.

On the inside... I was miserable.

The heaviness of being successful left me yearning for the lightness of being a beginner again, and this is where the self-sabotage began. I knew that as long as I had a Plan B, which was a business that took care of all my wants and needs financially, I would never follow through with Plan A, which was to create a business that would light me up every day.

Too many of us are slaves to our lifestyle. We build a business (or career) that we hate, to enable us to buy things we don't need, to impress people we don't even like. This is the paradox.

Throughout the later months of 2011 and the beginning half of 2012 I made the conscious decision to scale my multi-million dollar business down to zero. It felt like the only way to close this chapter of my life so that I could start over from scratch.

Unfortunately luck wasn't on my side. Two things, both beyond my control, happened during that time that became the nails in the coffin of my plan to ease myself out of the business. When the dust settled I realized that I would start the next chapter of my life with my soon-to-be wife and six month-old daughter with no business, no cash-flow, and a quarter of a million dollars of debt. I dig into my whole story online - bit.ly/JaysonStory

# "DON'T KILL YOURSELF."

*"Don't kill yourself" is one of the 100 rules for being an entrepreneur, written by my good friend James Altucher. It may sound extreme, but thoughts of suicide in the entrepreneurial community are more common than you might think. Many people dream about owning a company and the freedom of being their own boss - but even the most wonderful dreams can become nightmares.*

People don't realize that entrepreneurship is "living a few years of your life like most people won't, so you can spend the rest of your life like most people can't." The simple fact is that many entrepreneurs are constantly working through moments of near-debilitating anxiety and despair, just trying to make it by in times when it seems as though everything might crumble down around them.

As my friend Colin Collard once said, "When one door closes, another one opens, but it sucks to be stuck in the hallway." Transition is hard.

# THE
# BUTTERFLY EFFECT

*In October of 2012 a friend of mine offered an extra ticket to an intimate gathering with Seth Godin in New York for free on Facebook. Having very little obligations at the time, I jumped at the opportunity. Although I wasn't aware of it initially, the theme of the gathering was the "connection economy," or the theory that there is tremendous value in being the catalyst connecting like-minded individuals. The idea was simple but it fundamentally changed my mindset on relationship building.*

Many times throughout the event I caught myself thinking that there is no life path quite as isolating as entrepreneurship because everyone always works in their own little silos. When I returned home, I decided to start Mastermind Dinners.

For my first dinner I invited eight entrepreneurs who didn't know each other (but in my opinion should) and helped facilitate connecting them.

Truth be told I almost cancelled it two hours prior because I had almost convinced myself that no one would see the value in it. I was sure these people would think that I had wasted their time.

The little voice in my head, however, reminded me to get comfortable with the uncomfortable and let my discomfort guide me.

Thankfully it was too late to cancel and the dinner turned out to be a big success. The conversation didn't skip a beat for over four hours and for the first time in a long time, I genuinely lost track of time.

One particular moment from this first dinner will stay with me forever: about fifteen minutes in, one of my guests turned to another and said "You and I need to talk." When I overheard those words I had instant clarity that connecting people was something I wanted to do, in some capacity, for the rest of my life.

And so, without much clue as to where they would lead me I continued with these dinners. Although I had no "direct" financial benefit putting them on, I saw so much value being created I knew it was bound to come back to me someday. These dinners added onto my existing debt given that I was spending between $600-$800 each time, but deep down inside I knew that the bank could take my car, they could take whatever measly assets I had left, but they couldn't take my relationships.

Investing in my relationships was the safest investment I could make, and I believe the same is true for you.

# LEVERAGING
# EUSTRESS

*A few months following my first Mastermind Dinner I had an opportunity to do an event with Tim Ferriss. I felt like this was a chance for me to do what I was already doing in these dinners but on a larger scale. I never imagined that I would be in the event space, but as I said from the stage at our first MastermindTalks event, ignorance and confidence can go a long way when you're an entrepreneur.*

I 've always known that I work best with my back against the wall. I learned early on that if you don't stretch yourself in life, life (and business) will find a way to stretch you.

November 15th, 2012 I woke up early and saw a Facebook post from Tim entitled *"The 4-Hour Chef All-You-Can-Eat Campaign of Goodness."* The campaign was designed to sell bundles of books to the masses. The reason? Tim was the first author to publish through Amazon, and because of this Barnes and Noble tried to make an example of him by banning his book from their over 1,100 bookstores.

This put Tim in a big pinch; up until that point, all of his previous books were major best-sellers. Eliminating a large part of the physical retail from the equation for his newest release was going to be a problem... a major one.

Tim, being one of the smartest book marketers I know, created bundles where he offered one "Hail Mary" package for 4,000 books with the perk being that he would do two keynote talks anywhere in Canada or the United States.

When I first saw this package I thought of my good friend Scott who runs these huge entrepreneur events with 1500+ people. I knew that he would love to have Tim on his stage and could also easily give away (or sell) the books to his attendees. So I decided to send him an email. But the minute I clicked send I thought this could be a great opportunity for anyone, as Tim rarely does speaking engagements. So at 6:30 in the morning (less than two hours after he made the post) I emailed Tim directly, saying that I would buy the 4,000 books. The only problem being that I had nowhere near the money to pay for them.

The cost of the package was $84,000 and the window of opportunity for me was very short. I had to raise the money in less than two days. No easy feat when you've never raised money before (my last business was completely built on credit cards) and been programmed since you were a child to never ask for, or accept, hand outs.

That same morning I sent out a quick email to three friends. The first one wanted to talk about the numbers (projections, etc.), the second wanted to start a new business venture together, and the third offered to straight up loan me the money no questions asked. I chose the third option.

At the time of asking I had nothing aside from $250,000 of debt and a foggy business idea. I was in pure survival mode.

Recently when I asked this friend why he loaned me the money his answer was extremely clear: he wasn't investing in the business, he was investing in me.

This is why I say that it's so important not to tarnish your word, and always invest in your network. In the end they're all you have.

# MASTERMIND TALKS

*A few months later and the first MastermindTalks event was a huge success. My goal was to put 100 incredible entrepreneurs in a room for two days and facilitate connecting them. From the launch of the event in March to the actual event date in May we received over 4,200 applications from entrepreneurs all over the world. I wanted the right people in the room so I went through every single application one by one. I held phone calls with everyone who purchased a ticket and refunded those I didn't believe would be the right fit.*

The definition of an "entrepreneur" is quite vague, so deciding who is the 'right fit' for the event is difficult. Traditionally "entrepreneur" was a title held for those who had businesses with traditional overhead (staff, office leases, etc.). Now, because of technology, the business landscape has changed. Some of the most fascinating entrepreneurs in my network run beautifully well-oiled multi-million dollar businesses from anywhere in the world through their laptop. Using business size or revenues to determine an entrepreneur isn't the best marker either as revenues and profits scale very differently.

In the end, the deciding factor I choose to use is the least scientific of all. At the end of each phone call I ask myself "Is this someone I would want to have dinner with?", which takes me right back to where it all started: Mastermind Dinners.

If the answer is no I refund their ticket. And I did so for over a dozen people for our first event (totaling over $43,000). At the time I was still very much in debt and didn't know if that level of quality control would pay off or not. But it did... big time.

A testimonial left by one of the attendees sums it up best : "MastermindTalks felt like an enlightening two-day long dinner party in good company."

At our last two events we've been fortunate to host some brilliant minds - from Tim Ferriss and A.J. Jacobs (both multi-*NYT* Best-selling Authors), to James Altucher (Serial Entrepreneur and Best-selling Author), Ryan Holiday (Media Manipulator and Director of Marketing at American Apparel), Mike McDerment (Founder of Freshbooks), Dave Asprey (Founder of Bulletproof Coffee and the Bulletproof Exec), Aubrey Marcus (Founder of the Human Optimization Brand Onnit), Guy Kawasaki (Former Chief Evangelist at Apple), and many more.

Now, I want to be clear that I am not sharing my story to impress you. I am sharing it to impress upon you that we overestimate what we can accomplish in a day, but underestimate what we can accomplish in a year. Virtually all facets of my life are unrecognizable from where they were just a year ago, and I attribute that to surrounding myself with great people. I can sincerely say that I've never felt wealthier or more fulfilled. And I am definitely nothing special. I wasn't born into money, I wasn't born into power, and I wasn't labelled "gifted" as a child. Hell I dropped out of high school. But everything I have done can be replicated, and this book was created to show you how.

# A MUCH-NEEDED
# MINDSET SHIFT

*Much of the "networking" information space is about tools, tactics and strategies. In my opinion, those who focus all their energy on the mechanics of networking are missing the mark. Relationship building (or networking) is a mindset that stems from a deep caring for others. Tools and tactics (which you will learn in this book) simply amplify that.*

T he "money is the root of all evil" debate always makes me laugh. At the end of the day, money is a truth drug that simply amplifies who you are. If you're an asshole, the more money you make, the more of an asshole you'll most likely be.

Ryan Holiday spoke at our first MastermindTalks event, and the central idea of his talk was that if your product is crap, good marketing will just help people realize your product is crap quicker than they would have otherwise.

The same idea applies to relationship building; it doesn't matter what tools you use or how good your strategies are... if you're inauthentic, selfish, or egotistical, good strategies will just allow others to discover who you really are more quickly.

In this next chapter I want to 'set the table' by putting you in the mindset of a "connector," and shedding some light on who you need to become in order to build genuine and authentic relationships.

# ABUNDANCE
# VERSUS SCARCITY

*Abundance creates energy, and envy (scarcity) drains it. You need to surround yourself with people who are batteries and not black holes.*

I f you don't have an abundance mindset (or plan to adopt one) put this book down now because nothing I say in the next few pages will work for you. A scarcity mindset is zero-sum. It's a mindset that says there is only so much available in the world for everybody, and that everything needed for future survival and progress is either getting scarce or running out. If someone does well, it must be at the expense of everyone else who is doing poorly. Those who have a scarcity mindset look at relationships as transactional - "I do XYZ for you, and then I get to ask for something in return."

But here's the truth… a candle loses nothing by lighting another candle.

I have some amazing friends (who are also incredibly successful). The only reason that I do is because when they succeed, I cheer for them. I'm thrilled for them. I don't say to myself "Why do they have that, and I don't?" I know that I have different plans and energies and I'm not committed to doing the same things. If I was committed to the same things, I know I could probably accomplish similar results.

If you hear about someone's success and you aren't euphoric about it - if you're angry, hurt or there is a feeling of tightness inside of you, you've just guaranteed that you'll never reach that same level of success. If you resent someone else for being successful you teach your brain that striving for success is a bad thing for you to do.

# THE CONNECTION
# FORMULA

*Honesty, vulnerability and integrity are expensive gifts, don't expect them from cheap people.*

If you don't have honesty you can't have connection. As best-selling author and educator Stephen Covey once said, "trust is the glue of life. It's the most essential ingredient in effective communication. It's the foundational principle that holds all relationships together."

If you don't have the courage to be vulnerable at times you'll never be able to reach a real level of depth in your relationships. If you don't share your struggles, people won't buy your successes.

And lastly, if you don't have integrity, you have nothing. As Warren Buffett says, it takes twenty years to build a reputation and five minutes to ruin it. If you think about building your relationships like that you'll do things differently.

# BE A
# TALENT SCOUT

*Most people want to be connected with the Tim Ferriss',*
*Richard Branson's and Elon Musks of the world. The truth is*
*that they're at the top... and there is a lot of noise at the top.*
*These people are not looking for new friends or supporters.*
*Often times, if you're being honest with yourself, your moti-*
*vation to connect with big name people stems from ego.*

Admittedly, this was my focus early on in my career. Now I see it for what it is and connecting with big names just doesn't excite me anymore. What I love now is spotting talent, finding the real diamonds in the rough.

Recognizing someone with incredible potential, becoming their biggest fan or supporter, and watching them blow up is one of my greatest joys.

I wish that I could buy people at what they think they're worth, and sell them at their true worth.

Invest in people like others would invest in a business; the return is far greater.

# STOP COLLECTING AND START
# CONNECTING

*In a world where people measure their self worth by how many Facebook friends they have, I urge you to seek depth (quality) and not breadth (quantity) in your relationships. Look at your network like one of the most feared military forces in history, the Spartans. It was said that one Spartan was worth several men of any other state.*

I see almost everything in my business and life in the same vane. I would rather have a closed Facebook community of 500 members for my podcast than an email list of 5,000. I would rather have 150 people at a MastermindTalks event, where I know every attendee intimately, than have an event twice the size and barely know anyone by name. I would rather have intimate relationships with the vital few than the trivial many.

My philosophy is very much in alignment with Kevin Kelly's 1,000 True Fans theory. Tim Ferriss introduced this theory to me a few years ago and it has been incredibly impactful. The thesis of the 1,000 True Fans theory is that a creator, such as an artist, musician, photographer, craftsperson, performer, animator, designer, video maker, or author – in other words, anyone producing works of art – needs to acquire only 1,000 true fans to make a living.

I've noticed this theory rings true time and time again. Take a look at Kickstarter, a platform that virtually everyone is familiar with. At the end of the day Kickstarter is essentially a hub of interactions between creators and their true fans. The beautiful thing about it is that they are very transparent about their statistics. Out of 185,751 projects launched, 40.56% successfully funded, 1.37 billion dollars in pledges, etc. If we dig into the "successful" campaigns, there were 7,272,782 backers. Meaning the average amount of backers (7,272,782) per successful campaign (72,508) comes out to roughly only 100 backers per successful campaign. This number often shocks people as the perception is that you need thousands of supporters, but time and time again, the data shows this isn't the case at all.

So my question to you is, are you focused on depth or breadth in your relationships? Quality or quantity? At the end of the day it's not how many friends you can count, but how many friends you can count on.

# WOULD YOU BE FRIENDS WITH YOU?

A common mental exercise in the dating world is to ask "would you date yourself?" If you're single and seeking a confident, independent, physically fit partner... look in the mirror. If you're a lazy, overweight gamer living in your parents basement - good luck with that. Like attracts like. What I like to propose to people who want to improve their network is the idea that if you want to connect with someone who's a millionaire - what would make you interesting to a millionaire?

This idea doesn't have to be rooted in business success. There's no need to compete as there are various facets to life. Generally people are stronger in one area then they are in others. So my question to you is, what is your area of expertise? What's your unique ability?

Maybe it's time you did a personal balance sheet. Entrepreneurs list their assets and liabilities for their business on a regular basis, so why not do it for yourself on a personal level? List your strengths, weaknesses, what makes you unique, and the ways you can provide value to others. Doing so will give you a clear understanding of the ways you can be interesting to someone who you're hoping to connect with.

# Still not that interesting?

Well as the Chinese proverb says "The best time to plant a tree is twenty years ago, the second best time is now." Work on building your story. There are things that I do in my life specifically to have a better story. When opportunities come my way to do something I often ask myself if when my wife is reading my eulogy will all she be able to say is that I was a "good husband, father, and friend who lived a very comfortable and uneventful life?" That thought scares the crap out of me, and I don't want to leave my eulogy to chance. I jump at most opportunities that will lead to a better story, or a better life lived.

# GETTING COMFORTABLE WITH THE UNCOMFORTABLE

*If I could boil my success down to one thing it's that I have always surrounded myself with people who were one or two steps ahead of me. My model has always been that if you're the smartest person in the room you're in the wrong room. Surrounding yourself with people who will make you feel uncomfortable (on some level) forces you to grow as quickly as possible to bridge the gap between where you are and where they are.*

As human beings, we have a deep need to belong and to feel accepted. Ten thousand years ago, if you didn't belong and weren't accepted within a tribe you would die. You would either starve or get eaten by an animal bigger than you. One of the only reasons we've survived as a species is due to our ability to band together in numbers. Even though our environment has changed, this deep need to belong is a survival mechanism that isn't going away anytime soon. When you understand this you can use it to your advantage.

Get comfortable with the uncomfortable because un-faced fears become your limits. Surround yourself with people who make you feel uncomfortable on some level. If you do, it's a great indication that you're growing in ways you may not even be aware of. When we choose to surround ourselves with people who are playing at a level or two above us it unconsciously drives us to strive to get to that level as soon as possible. All growth begins at the end of your comfort zone.

Who you surround yourself with is who you become, so choose wisely.

# MASTERMIND DINNERS

_Now let's dive into the highest value "connecting" activity that I do: Mastermind Dinners._

I believe something magical happens when you put brilliant minds and unconventional thinkers together in a room. Because of this I try to host gatherings at every opportunity, and they often take the form of dinners. I break these 'Dinners' down into two categories: local dinners and location dinners. Both are generally focused around three areas:

( 1 ) **RECONNECTING WITH OLD TIES.** (Catching up, and keeping relationships healthy)

( 2 ) **INTRODUCING PEOPLE WHO CAN BENEFIT FROM KNOWING EACH OTHER.** (There is a lot of strategic thought behind this)

( 3 ) **Connecting with people who I've been meaning to connect with for quite some time.** (Killing eight birds with one stone, in essence)

Often, Mastermind Dinners can be a mix of all three categories. With that said, you have to be very conscious of the synergy of the group.

Local dinners are exactly what you think - dinners you host in your local area. They enable you to build 'roots' locally and they also give you the benefit of having a "go to" restaurant that you can make use of on a regular basis which is nice from a logistics perspective. At the same time, however, a local dinner can make it harder to get schedules to align.

Location dinners are my favorite to host. They are great to do when you want to reconnect with old ties when travelling, or to connect people with a common interest. A great example is to hold these when you go to another city for an event. Holding a dinner around an event is often the easiest to host for three reasons:

( 1 ) **First,** people who are going to an event share some form of common interest by default.

( 2 ) **Second,** many events will offer a list of attendees or some sort of access to an online community before the event, so it's easy to create a list of people to reach out to.

( 3 ) **AND FINALLY,** you're catching people outside their natural routine. Many people may eat dinner at home, do yoga Wednesday nights, have date night with their spouse on Fridays, etc. Hosting a dinner for a bunch of people who are travelling is an easy way to stay clear of the normal day-to-day routines, commitments, and responsibilities they may have.

# EVEN LEADERS NEED
# A TRIBE

*Want to supercharge your networking with real players?*
*Hold a dinner for speakers. Everyone has a yearning to be*
*connected to like-minded individuals and speakers are not*
*exempt from that rule. Event producers rarely do anything*
*for their speakers while in town so it's very easy to throw*
*something together and be a hero. Again, you're catching*
*them outside of their natural routine, but you're also catch-*
*ing them outside of their natural behavior of saying 'no' to*
*something like this by default.*

# WHY?

BJ Fogg has a philosophy that if you drastically change your environment you drastically change your behavior. Saying 'no' is often an

unconscious behavioral response. Therefore, you're often more likely to get a 'yes' to a request like this when someone is travelling.

# Planning the Perfect
# Dinner

*A perfect dinner starts with perfect planning. Here are a few things to keep in mind when planning your dinner:*

## Commonalities

You must be sure there is at least one commonality amongst your guests. It could be that they are all entrepreneurs, athletes, artists... it doesn't matter, but there has to be one unifying area of conversation. Having said that, there are two areas of concern when looking for this commonality:

First, make sure you don't select people at both extremes of the unifying commonality. You don't want to have an entrepreneur with a one-hundred million dollar company at a dinner with a bunch of people who have startups. Occasionally it may work, but you really don't want to leave the synergy of a dinner to chance. People yearn to surround themselves with like-minded individuals and there is a big difference in the wants, needs, and pains of a one-hundred million dollar company and a startup.

Second, you don't want to invite anyone with a conflicting interest (i.e. direct competitors). The goal for you as a dinner host is to put four to eight incredible people in a room and create an environment where they feel comfortable to open up and share. If you have two direct competitors in the same room there is a good chance the conversation won't flow as well as it could have, so be very conscious of this.

I'll talk more about commonalities a little later in the book.

# GROUP SIZE

O ver the years I have tested many different group sizes and have found that different group sizes serve different purposes. Dinners can be as structured or organic as you want. I tend to prefer table sizes of four to six people. The smaller the group size, the more intimate the dinner feels, the more ground you can cover, and there's an all around better chance there will be a flow to the conversation.

Four Guests: Groups of four are great! A table size like this ensures intimacy and that everyone will have an opportunity to talk. Due to the level of intimacy you need to make sure there will be great synergy amongst your guests. If there is a bad fit at the table it can really put a damper on the entire conversation. Also if someone cancels last minute (which does happen), having three people is a little awkward as a table set up, and the flow of the conversation will most definitely be impacted.

FIVE GUESTS: Groups of five are great because if you do end up with a last minute cancellation it doesn't impact your dinner as much. However, in a group of five, you may want to sit at the end and play more of a facilitator role as the uneven number of guests gives you the chance to guide the conversations should you need to.

SIX GUESTS: In groups of six you should consider moving to a round table set up. Having six people at a traditional style table starts to make things difficult from a noise perspective (not impossible, just a little more difficult). Also in a group of this size, you will need to take on more of a facilitator role as you'll usually have one or two people dominate the conversation.

EIGHT GUESTS OR MORE: In a group of eight or more you'll most likely need to start looking into a private dining room. Although I host dinners of this size from time to time they are generally not my favorite for several reasons. The first is of course cost. As I mentioned above, for groups of eight or more you generally need a private room so that everyone can hear each other, and private rooms are not cheap.

The second concern is facilitation. You need to play the role of observer and facilitator. Managing the flow of conversation at a dinner of this size is a full time job.

Third is the possibility of regret. I've been to dinners of eight or more where I'm at one side of the table and I'm trying to listen to and participate in the conversation at the other end. This often leaves you discounting the people you are sitting with and wishing you were seated somewhere else.

And fourth is intimacy. In a dinner group of eight or more there is a very good chance that there will be two or three conversations going on simultaneously. It's hard to concentrate on the conversation you're in when there are other interesting conversations going on at the same time. One way around this is to suggest a change of seating mid-way through the dinner. This may or may not work well (because it may interrupt the flow of conversation), but it is an option if you are trying to get everyone to know everyone else.

*DINNER SIZES MENTIONED ABOVE INCLUDE YOU THE DINNER HOST / FACILITATOR

# FINDING DINNER GUESTS

*At a recent large dinner I hosted in NYC I sent out thirty four invitations. Out of that group, thirty two people said yes and showed up to that dinner with not a single cancellation. That's a 94% acceptance rate on a dinner that consisted of multiple New York Times bestselling authors, online influencers and well-known industry leaders. I say this because two years ago this definitely wasn't the response I was getting. I was lucky to get a 5% response rate to my invites and had to deal with several last minute cancellations on more than one occasion.*

What changed? Social proof. And the only way to get social proof is by putting in the work. Sean Stephenson says that "if you want to experience success, be prepared to face dead-ends and false-alarms. They're meant to shake off wannabes." So start small. Run a few dinners with some "not so big" names. Get your feet wet, get comfortable. I still get nervous before every single one of my dinners, but that feeling is lessened with every dinner that I hold.

Before brainstorming who you would like to invite be clear as to "why" you are putting on these dinners in the first place, and why you want certain individuals there. There is no wrong answer, but just be clear. I will preface this by saying that a warm outreach is always better than a cold one. When I started doing dinners I was really building my network from scratch, so I decided to use a local business magazine award list to brainstorm people to invite. This was an uphill battle because I had no influence or social proof and was reaching out to these people cold. I recommend that you learn from my mistakes and avoid trying to reach out to people cold. Playing along the lines of what we touched on earlier, we all have a desire to be connected to like-minded individuals. It's important to share a commonality with someone you're reaching out to.

A commonality you can use to your advantage could also be a mutual friend. Conventional wisdom says we are six degrees from anyone. With the rise of social media, I would argue that the gap has closed significantly. In most circles you'll see that you are almost always one degree of separation from someone else. If there is someone you don't know directly who you would like to invite, check Facebook or Linkedin. You may have some common contacts that you can either use for an introduction or to leverage their name when doing the outreach.

- **A COMMONALITY COULD BE AN ORGANIZATION** like EO, YEC, or Vistage. It could also be a meetup.com group.

- **A COMMONALITY COULD BE A PLATFORM** like FoundersCard, Clarity.fm, or a closed Facebook group.

- **A COMMONALITY COULD BE AN EVENT.** Again, it's often easy to get an attendee list in advance.

The possibilities really are endless!

The exception to rule is that the commonality does not need to be between you and your guests, it can be amongst the guests themselves. If you want to host a dinner for best-selling authors, once you get the first two or three on board, you can then authentically position it as a dinner for best-selling authors.

# TARGETED VS SPRAY AND PRAY

There are two schools of thought when it comes to sending invitations for something like dinners. The first is to spray and pray, essentially sending an email blast out to a bunch of people to see who will sign up. The second is a much more targeted and methodical approach. I genuinely care about the synergy at the table so I've always chosen the latter.

# The Food Chain and Anchored Tenants

If sending targeted invites is the direction you choose to go, working up the food chain and anchor tenants are two powerful concepts you should put into use. Looking back I believe I may have learned the "working up the food chain" philosophy from Ryan Holiday's *Trust Me I'm Lying* book trailer. The book is based in media and public relations, but the tactic can easily be used in a networking setting. The methodology is to start small. His advice is to send your story to a small personal blog from an alias email - you get an exclusive, and they get an outlet. You then take that exclusive link and send another anonymous email to a larger site. Like links in a chain you start to move your story to larger and more influential sites until eventually your story becomes the story and you're featured in a major publication.

I'll give you an example of this approach as it applies to hosting Mastermind Dinners. Let's say you want to host a dinner for a group of speakers, and you have a list of ten prospects. Start small by inviting the person who would most likely give you a 'yes' (oftentimes this is the person who is least in "demand" and has the smallest influence). Once you get that person on board, move on to the second most likely person to give you a 'yes.' Similar to Ryan's approach, you work yourself up the chain, building social proof along the way.

The second approach to use when sending targeted invites is getting the big fish, also known as the anchor tenant, right away. Often this requires much more work and strategy, but as they say in the dating world; it's easier to pick up a single ten, than four eights because all of your energy is focused.

Unconsciously, I used both of these strategies to build MastermindTalks. Before our first event I was a complete nobody. I had little to no influence, and virtually no brand. When the opportunity to do the event with Tim fell into my lap I knew that I could use him as an anchor to get others to speak (especially those who wanted to be connected to him). The event could also be a catalyst for re-connecting him with all of his friends.

I didn't realize it at the time, but this approach has a nice by product of helping to build credibility by association. Even though I've never written a best-selling book or have done anything on an 'influencer' capacity, there is a kind of 'rub off effect' where you build credibility and influence almost through osmosis. If people trust or are influenced by someone like a James Altucher or a Tim Ferriss and I'm friends with them (and am often seen in their circles), then that same trust and influence rubs off on me.

# AUTHENTIC
# MARKETING 101

*Celebrated TED speaker Simon Sinek says "people don't buy what you do, they buy why you do it." This small piece of wisdom was literally all that I had when launching our first MastermindTalks event. I didn't have a full roster of speakers, I didn't have brand momentum, and I certainly didn't have money for marketing. On top of all this, a lot of people thought the event was a scam.*

I wasn't selling the what, I was selling the why. I was transparent and authentic about why I was putting on the event, and why there was a need for it. Here's a link to the original sales video I created three years ago, simply using a webcam: http://bit.ly/mmt2013

I have a very different approach to marketing than most. I don't A/B test, I don't use cutting edge buzzwords or copy. As my friend Renee Airya says, "my heart is my sales letter."

A good salesman knows that his first real sale is himself. I've learned that when you're honest, raw and authentic, marketing is effortless. If people don't bite it's most likely because they are not the right fit, and I NEVER sell something to someone when they aren't the right fit. For those who are the right fit, no explanation is necessary. For those who are not the right fit, no explanation will do.

Traditional marketing is about posturing, being polished, and oftentimes stretching the truth. When making the move to authentic or transparent marketing, many people fear what others will think. Make no mistake, authenticity builds credibility. My good friend Michael Fishman sums it up perfectly when he says that "credibility can be established with credentials or by being transparent that you have no credentials."

That being said, there are no 'templates' I can really provide when practicing authentic marketing, because each and every circumstance is different. Every individual outreach will require a different opener, a different piece of social proof, a different angle. However, at the request of some of the people in our MMT community, I thought I would share some best practices around outreach to those who are typically unreachable.

# REACHING THE
# UNREACHABLE

*I have a very good track record of getting in touch with big names - because of a mix of many things. Creative outreach is one of the reasons I am so successful, and it is something you can easily leverage for yourself.*

There's a saying from the book *22 Immutable Laws of Marketing* (one of my favorite books of all time) that says "What works in the military works in marketing, and that's the unexpected." This is the guiding principle I use not only in a marketing context, but also when it comes to relationship building and outreach. If you're reaching out to someone they should be treated as a prospect on some level. You may not be reaching out to them for money, but you're reaching out for an even more precious commodity - their time. We live in a world where there are two currencies: money and time. That's why they call it "paying" attention. In a world that is increasingly more demanding of people's time, attention is the new currency.

Creatively cutting through the clutter is key when reaching out to high profile people. An attribute that all great marketers share is their ability to put themselves in their prospect's shoes. What is their model of the world? What does their average day look like? What are their wants, needs, and fears? A great marketer is often more aware of these things than the prospect is. Put yourself in your prospect's shoes: where are they when they receive your email? What other distractions or demands may be happening at that time?

Questioning your own motives is, again, very important. Before you do any kind of outreach to anyone, especially a big name, you must ask yourself "why?". Why are you reaching out to this particular person? What is the desired outcome? Be very clear. Also ask yourself, if I am unable to connect with this person, are there alternative people who could help me reach the same desired outcome? By widening your options you will realize there may be several people who you can contact instead who will help you get to exactly where you want to go, with a lot less effort. For example, if you want to reach out to a world-class swimmer for some high-level advice or guidance it would be much easier to reach out to a silver medalist instead of Michael Phelps. Both are among the best in the world, and both will most likely get you to where you want to go, but one would be much easier to reach out to than the other.

Don't forget to ask yourself one of the most important questions of all - "what is in it for them?" It is baffling how often this question is overlooked. If you're reaching out to someone cold, there must be some kind of clear benefit for them.

# DO YOUR RESEARCH

It is imperative that you know who you're reaching out to, inside and out. That's where the internet can become your very best friend - the more high profile the person, the more information you can find on them. Some questions to ask yourself are "what do they like?" "what do they dislike?" "what charities do they support?" By doing in-depth research you may be able to find a unique angle to use to reach out to that person. You may be reaching out for business purposes, but you may be able to connect based on a common interest outside of business. Doing so will greatly increase your chances of cutting through the noise and catching their attention.

# DO YOU HAVE ANY FRIENDS IN COMMON?

As I touched on earlier, in a society where we are continuously reacting to an increasing amount of stimulus, it has become harder to reach out to someone cold. Check platforms like Facebook and Linkedin to see if you have any mutual connections. If for some reason you don't find any common connections, broadcast out to your network. Every time I've done this I've had incredible success. I've connected with best-selling authors, well-known business figures, even a former astronaut just by using this strategy.

It doesn't hurt to ask!

# ASSESS THE NOISE

The last part of your research is assessing the least 'noisy' medium for outreach. As mentioned above, connecting through a mutual contact is always best, but if you are unable to do that you have many other methods over and above traditional email. Some of these methods include Facebook, Twitter, Linkedin, INmail, or even traditional direct mail. Although email is always a rather effective way to reach someone, it is often monitored by gatekeepers (personal assistants) which can hurt your chances of getting through.

If email is your chosen method, however, tracking down someone's email address can be the difficult part. Never fear - I have an awesome trick you can use that has helped me track down the email addresses of some of the biggest names. Unfortunately I can't walk you through it in this book because I need to visually show it to you. I've created a video explaining it for you in the resource page.

Generally the more expensive or creative the medium the better. Email was once very effective, but because there is no cost involved, it has been overused and abused by marketers; I get upwards of 100 emails a day. Email can be a very tough channel for outreach but there are other options if you're creative. For example, with the rise of email, there has been a huge decline in direct mail. As my good friend Brian Kurtz says, "the least cluttered mailbox is the one you grew up with." Receiving something in the mail has become novel, and is a great way to stand out.

# EFFORT AND STRATEGY

Now that we've laid the groundwork it's time to reach out. No matter what contact medium you choose, the success of the outreach is often in direct proportion to the amount of effort you put into it. Getting your message in front of someone isn't difficult. Getting them emotionally hooked and eliciting a response from them is. Over the years I've learned that people will reward effort. If you send an email to someone with very little research, very little personalization, and an unclear ask, you've done more harm than good. Conversely, if you put a lot of effort into really personalizing your approach you'll have a much better chance of eliciting a response.

Because email is the most common medium for outreach, I will give you an example of an approach:

# SUBJECT LINE

It doesn't matter how much research you've done or how much effort you put into your email if the five or six words you use in the subject line of your message don't hook your prospect. Use your creative muscle and brainstorm a few options. Ask yourself, "If I received 500+ emails a day, would I bother to open this email?" Here are a few samples of email titles that I've used in the past:

"*Hey Tim, I'm in town on Tuesday…*"

"*Adam told me to reach out to you…*"

"*John, I'm doing a dinner with a group of entrepreneurs…*"

Notice how all the subject titles are open ended. An overwhelming amount of email subject lines are not open ended, so using an open ended subject line helps you cut through the noise. Also notice that they all elicit curiosity - "Adam told me to reach out to you…" Which Adam? Why did he tell you to reach out? "Hey Tim, I'm in town on Tuesday…" "Why are you in town?" "John, I'm doing dinner with a group of entrepreneurs" Who else is going? Leaving subject lines open can be a great hook.

Depending on your subject line your receivers may think your email is spam. To avoid this, try to include something specific to them. Using their name in the subject line can also be a rather powerful hook. Studies have shown that the sweetest sound in the human language is one's own name - why not leverage that? Having someone's name included in the title of the email is so rarely done, so it's another tactic to help you cut through the noise.

# BODY OF THE MESSAGE

T here really is no 'perfect' email. Every strategy is different because every outreach is different. There are, however, two formats I commonly use when reaching out to someone cold. The 9-word email and video email.

The 9-word email is a strategy I learned from Dean Jackson. It's designed to revive old leads, but it can be very useful in an initial outreach as well. The format of the email is just as it sounds, an email in nine words. The reason the strategy is so powerful is because it's very quick for the recipient to read, which in turn elicits a quick response. In a world where 65% of emails are read on a mobile device first, the shorter the response the prospect needs to give, the better. This strategy also allows you to leverage small wins. Never send someone a long drawn out email with many reasons for them to say no. Instead, build the conversation with simple wins. For example, if you send an email saying:

"*Hey Steve! You may remember me, I'm... (blah, blah, blah). I'm holding a dinner on Tuesday with 10 people, and XYZ restaurant at 7:30pm and wanted to know if you wanted to come...*"

There are a solid 3 - 4 reasons why Steve may say no to that email. Instead, you would be better positioned to say:

"*Hey Steve! I'm planning to hold a dinner next week with a group of ____ (Best-selling authors, entrepreneurs, artists, etc...), interested?*"

If he says 'yes' that's a small win. Then email #2 would include a date and a time. If you get a 'yes' to email #2, you can move on to #3. If you get an objection to the date or time in email #2, you are more clear on the objection than you would be otherwise and it gives you an opportunity to adjust your approach.

By eliciting only a tiny commitment off the bat you increase your chances of opening up dialogue, which is the core goal of reaching out in the first place. Also there's a cognitive bias in play here. Once somebody says 'yes' to something small, they're more likely to say the same thing when asked for something big in order to be congruent with their initial response.

# VIDEO OR AUDIO OUTREACH

T he second email I like to use for outreach is a video or audio email. Again, the success of the outreach is often in direct proportion to the amount of effort you put into it, and sending a video or audio email is a great way to stand out. I stumbled across this power of this tactic a few years ago. Contrary to the belief of many people I am very much an introvert when it comes to "networking." Historically, I tend to be the type that sits back and observes others when in a new social setting. In August of 2011 I attended a $10 000 two-day event filled with online influencers and best-selling authors. Knowing that the value of the event really came down to the people in the room, I was clear that I wanted to do everything I could to forge a relationship with these people well after the event. Six months later I sent personal videos to a select group of individuals from that event that I wanted to stay in touch with, and the response was overwhelming. Here's a quick snapshot of how powerful this form of outreach can be - http://bit.ly/videoreaction1 and http://bit.ly/video-reaction2

Since then, according to my Youtube account, I have sent over 1100+ personalized videos. There are several ways to do these videos and no fancy equipment is required. For more information, visit our resource page.

Now let's deal with two worst case scenarios:

# No Response

D id they receive the email? Did they not like it? Did they forget to reply? The unknown can be a killer. Not receiving a response is often worse than receiving a 'no.' Thankfully there are tools out there that you can use to help track when emails are opened. A tool that I use for Gmail is called Yesware.

If you can confirm that an email has been opened there are two strategies you can use to engage your prospect afterwards. The first is to restructure the email and provide a little more information (another benefit of not showing all your cards up front). And the second is to simply re-send the original email. Coming from someone who receives a couple hundred emails at a time in a single day, it's easy for an email to get lost in the clutter. Don't assume a lack of reply means they weren't interested.

# OBJECTIONS AND REJECTIONS

H ow you deal with a rejection or objection is really case-by-case. In most dinner invite scenarios, objections are generally timing related, so I'm very respectful of that. There's no point to emailing back other than to say "Thanks for getting back to me." If for some reason the prospect replies and says they don't see value, you'll want to take the approach case-by-case yet again. Warren Buffet once said that "the difference between successful people and really successful people is that really successful people say 'no' to almost everything". People with big names are very protective of their time, and with reason.

Although I would not make use of it in the particular instance, one great tip I got from my friend Craig Morantz, CEO at Kira Talent, is whenever faced with an objection follow up with a question like "Under what circumstances would you say yes?" The success I've had from posing this simple question has been astounding.

Let's say you're trying to get a lunch meeting with someone and they give you a straight out 'no,' with no real context. By posing the question above, it puts the onus on the other person to clarify what a 'yes' would look like. Maybe they can't do lunch but they can do a coffee. Maybe they can't do coffee but they can do a call. Maybe they can't schedule anything right now because of time demands, but they could the following month. Oftentimes the difference between a 'yes' and a 'no' is a ridiculously small concession.

There is a lot of effort and strategy that goes into 'reaching the unreachable.' The two most important things to remember are putting yourself in the shoes of your prospect and that conventional methods of outreach will yield conventional results. First impressions are very important, so don't let your outreach be "just another email."

As Wayne Gretzky says "you miss 100% of the shots you don't take," so you'll never know if you don't try. The bigger the name the higher the chance you will get a 'no,' so don't be afraid to start small. It's nice to be connected to the big names of the world, but it's just as important to remember that the best network is the one you already have.

I'm in a phase of my life where I have little desire to expand my network. I have incredible people in my life and limited bandwidth. I'm currently in a much better position to go deep with my existing relationships then to find new ones. Often when hosting a dinner (especially when travelling), I'll use programs like connect.com, contactually. com, or LinkedIn search to find out who in my network lives in the city I am visiting. Should I want to hold a dinner with some new people, I may make a post to Facebook saying something like "Travelling to San Diego, do you have anybody you think I should connect with while I'm in town?" These are the most common ways I fill my dinners now, and they work famously!

# THE MAGIC IS IN THE DETAILS

## CHOOSING THE PERFECT RESTAURANT

*I put a TON of thought into choosing a restaurant for my Mastermind Dinners. The beautiful thing about hosting dinners locally is that once you have one or two go-to restaurants it's a huge weight off your shoulders logistically. Also if you bring a consistent stream of business to a restaurant, they will treat you like gold and there are other ways you can leverage the relationship (including some kind of discount, financial kickback, or concessions). In contrast, for a recent location dinner in NYC, my assistant spent over seven hours trying to find a restaurant that would work for our specific group (just as a side note, we decided on The Meatball Shop in Chelsea and it was FANTASTIC).*

Be conscious of the wants and needs of your guests when picking a restaurant. Consider everything from location, menu diversity (I usually try to find restaurants that are vegetarian, and Paleo-friendly), meal cost, noise level, availability of private rooms (and private room minimums), all the way down to the table location. If I don't know a restaurant first-hand and can't select a table in advance it's not uncommon for me to show up a little over an hour early to pick the perfect spot.

# Pre-Dinner and Prep

Do you have your restaurant picked? Do you have dinner guests lined up? Now it's time for the real work. Don't get lazy, this is where the magic happens. I can't hit the next point hard enough.

# Do Your Research (Again!)

A networker does research on companies; a relationship builder does research on people. This is key, especially when hosting a dinner. There are two schools of thought around how much research is needed. I will present them both to you and you can decide what resonates most for you.

The first school of thought is to do the bare minimum required when it comes to research in order to be respectful (their name, their business, what they do). There are benefits of going into the dinner blind. One, it forces you to be present. Two, it forces you to ask very poignant and interesting questions because your brain hasn't been formatted with someone's Wikipedia page. If you do a ton of research on an individual it may feel like the conversation has already been "had," which can make things very stale. It's the difference between connecting with the person vs the persona.

The second school of thought is that a host should know as much about the group as possible in advance. The more you know the better. Knowing their name and business simply isn't enough because you don't want to leave the serendipity of great conversations to chance. Do research on their business, their ideal client, the names of their children, what they like, and what keeps them up at night.

There are two reasons for this:

(1) **FIRST,** a connector is primed to see connections and to leverage his or her network to solve problems for others. If I know someone is having an issue with culture in their business, I will sit them down next to someone who has rockstar culture in theirs.

(2) **SECOND,** when you take your research to this next level, you are

then able to harness the power of uncommon commonalities, and that is how deep connections are forged.

Let me give you an example of how uncommon commonalities work.

Say you're at a table of business owners. Business owners represent only 3% of the general population. That's an uncommon commonality right there. Let's take it a bit further and say you're at a dinner with a group of business owners with seven-figure businesses - they represent the top 4% of all business owners. That's an even stronger uncommon commonality. Or maybe it's a group of business owners with businesses with 50+ million in revenue - they are the top 0.04% of business owners.

The deeper the uncommon commonality the deeper the bond. As I've said many times before, we all have a deep desire to be connected to like-minded individuals. This trait goes beyond business in obvious ways. Perhaps the uncommon commonality is that your dinner guests are parents, they served in the military, or have a love of travel. Whatever it is, discovering uncommon commonalities through research will enable you to steer into deep and bonding conversations with your dinner guests.

Some rudimentary level of research is required regardless of the route you go, but the amount of depth you chose to go with it is completely up to you.

# PRE-DINNER COMMUNICATION

U pon acceptance of the dinner invitation I send a calendar invite with all of the specifics. I frequently get asked if I share the list of guests with attendees. Many people do, but I generally tend not to because it can lead to false perceptions and expectations. If some guests research other guests beforehand they will often pre-judge the quality of the dinner or the attendees based on their online presence. Although your professional life is often a collection of stuff from the web it's not the best marker of someone's 'success' (I know many people with high-figure businesses who have virtually no online identity). I used to do this myself but I've learned to reserve my judgement because I've been proven wrong so many times. As James Altucher says "You never know what someone is worth until they declare bankruptcy."

Often the people you think are 'successful' aren't, and the ones who you think aren't, are. Never believe the smoke and mirrors.

The night before the dinner I send a very quick reminder email with all the pertinent details (time, restaurant, address, and a link to a Google map) and my cell phone number should they need to let me know if they'll be late or if something comes up.

# WHO PICKS UP THE TAB?

D eciding this far in advance is very important. It can be extremely awkward when a server comes to the table and asks if you want separate checks when you haven't discussed anything with your dinner guests in advance. There are a few different payment options that you can make use of:

# Host Pay

Almost all of the dinners I host are covered by me. If I am the one inviting people for dinner I always pay. According to best-selling author Robert Cialdini it builds reciprocity, which is always nice, but that's not why I do it. It is simply the way I have done it in the past and will continue to do in the future. Another option to cut the cost is to cohost your dinner with someone who values networking as much as you do. My friends Michael Fishman and Ramit Sethi hosted an awesome monthly dinner series in New York together for two years.

# User Pay

Most people are fine with picking up their own tab (and many want to). If this is the route you would like to go you can either make mention of it in the original invite email (by referring to the dinner as a "dutch treat"), or you can set up a quick Eventbrite page to take payment in advance. If you're intending to host your Mastermind Dinners for monetary purposes then this is the route you would go. A by product of using Eventbrite is that it guarantees the people attending are 'invested' in the dinner which makes them much less likely to cancel last minute.

# SPONSOR PAY

Finding a company who is willing to sponsor your dinners is a great option as well. Now that I have MastermindTalks you could say that my company sponsors mine. It's a GREAT investment from a business ROI perspective. For roughly $10,000 I can host almost 25 dinners, connecting and re-enforcing existing ties with over 150 amazing people. In my last business I wouldn't think twice about spending $10,000 on marketing with no guaranteed return. The value of these dinners, however, is utterly incredible! Your network is truly your net worth.

# WANT TO MAKE YOUR DINNER FUN?

Credit Card Roulette is something I do from time to time with groups that I know well. Everyone at the table puts their credit card in a pile and hands them to the waiter who then puts them into a napkin or glass. The waiter pulls out the cards one by one, and the last card removed is stuck taking care of the bill. It's really a lot of fun to play and definitely makes the dinner memorable. The key is telling your guests in advance and allowing people who want to pay for their own bill to opt out.

Another fun game is Phone Stacking. When at a dinner, people are often on their phones - so grab them and stack them face down in the center of the table. The first to pick up their phone pays the bill for all. Have fun with your guests, and do things to really make your dinner memorable.

# ASSIGNED SEATING

T he last thing to consider before the dinner itself is whether or not you will prepare a seating arrangement in advance. This isn't worth considering should you be hosting a gathering for four or five people. With larger groups there are some benefits to planning your seating in advance. First, you can pair people up based on synergy or uncommon commonalities. Second, I've been on the guest side of a Mastermind Dinner and there's always that moment of the paradox of choice that one experiences. Having your seating arranged in advance can help alleviate the worry associated with a guest 'choosing the right spot.' This is yet 'another thing to worry about' but caring is the ultimate competitive advantage. I'm reminded of Wayne Dyer's saying "go the extra mile, it's never crowded." I do assigned seating for our Master-mindTalks events (150 people) and switch up the seating four times during each event. The planning behind that takes days.

My good friend Dan Martell runs similar dinners which are more organic, and he does something he calls 'Table Searing.' He always tries "to sit the most interesting and outgoing person near the center of the table so everyone can easily hear them." He also always tries to sit in the center position so that he can act like a "conversation cop" to "pull people into the conversation." There really is no right or wrong, it just comes down to personal preference.

# YOUR MASTERMIND
# DINNER

*It's the day of your dinner, congrats!*

I t's almost show time. The hard work is done, but there are two last things I like to do before the dinner begins that I feel you should do as well. First, I call the restaurant to confirm the reservation. Then, a few hours before I send a personal text message to the attendees, which serves as check-in and quick reminder. It's often appreciated, and a bonus is that they now have your phone number readily available should they be late for any reason. Second, I usually arrive at the restaurant anywhere between 25 to 60 minutes in advance to ensure we get the right table (if I've not been able to select our table in advance). Also, should anyone arrive early, I'll be there to greet them. Depending upon the restaurant layout and if you're using a private room or not you can start drinks at the bar, or usher people right to the table. That's totally your call, but when everybody has arrived, it's time to kick off the dinner!

# KICKING OFF THE DINNER RIGHT

The initial introductions can be as casual or as structured as you want. I like to open by explaining my relationship with everyone at the table, and why everyone is there. I then like to follow up with some ground rules, which may include the following:

**CONFIDENTIALITY** - Confidentiality is a big thing, especially for entrepreneurs. Setting the tone that everything shared in the room should not leave the room will really help people open up and share. People often overlook setting this agenda at the beginning because they 'assume' people won't share outside of the dinner. Never assume.

**WINE BY THE GLASS** - "Are we ordering a bottle?" comes up at every dinner. I usually state in advance that everyone can order whatever they want but if it's wine, order by the glass. One of the major reasons is that if bottles of wine are on the table people will drink it. If they need to order by the glass, they won't order as much. This helps both to keep the cost down and lessen the possibility of someone having a little too much to drink (which can happen).

**NO CELL PHONES** - This is optional, but nothing drags a conversation down more than someone being on their phone the entire time.

**GET ORDERING OUT OF THE WAY** - I usually say that I want everybody to order within a few minutes of housekeeping and introductions because this can really drag on in a large dinner. It's not uncommon that an hour after the dinner has started, people are in such deep conversation that they have yet to look at the menu. It's happened to me several times, so don't forget to touch on this during your housekeeping.

END TIME - It's important to state an end time in advance. Sometimes you'll hit that three to four hour mark and people may need to leave but don't want to be seen as rude. State in advance that the dinner is done by 9:30pm (or whatever your set time is) but that everyone is more than welcome to stay longer. This allows those who need to leave early to do so gracefully while others can stick around.

Once you set the tone for the dinner, start with your formal introductions. You should go first because it's an opportunity for you to lead by example. The more open and vulnerable you can be during your introduction the more people will follow that vulnerability throughout, and the deeper the connections will be.

Vulnerability is the key to deep connections. Oftentimes in 'networking' settings it's a game of posturing and surface level B.S. You have an opportunity to create an environment of real and raw connections (and people will never forget you for it) so don't take this opportunity lightly.

Some intros I like to use include:

• TOP PROFESSIONAL OR BUSINESS ACHIEVEMENT (brag)

- **Top Personal Achievement** (brag)

- **A bold goal** (something they are trying to accomplish in the coming year)

- **"Thorns and roses"** - This is one of my favorite openers especially when you're dealing with business owners. You state something going well in your life or business (a rose), something that has the potential of being great (a bud), and something that is a pain (a thorn). This exercise forces people to open up a little more than a brag so some push back is to be expected sometimes (as far as people not going as deep as they could). As long as you go first people often open up pretty easily afterwards.

At our MastermindTalks events we do a lot of facilitated networking. And to do that we use some ice breaker cards, which include some of the examples below:

- *Complete this statement: "I lose track of time when…"*

- *What have you done in the past 3 months that makes you feel proud?*

- *As you have gotten older, what has become more important and less important to you?*

- *If you could study with any expert in the world, who would you work with and what would you study?*

- *If you could invite 3 people (living or dead) to your home for dinner, who would they be and why?*

(For the full list of 50 questions, visit the book resource page at MastermindDinners.com).

After the intros, conversation should start to flow pretty naturally, but this is where your job as a facilitator kicks in. Be conscious of people's body language at the table - people making pacifying gestures, who's dominating the conversation, who's not talking enough… there is no silver bullet to facilitation. Your role is simply to make sure that everyone shares stories and experiences, and thoroughly enjoys themselves. As long as you are observant and have a genuine care for those at the table facilitation takes care of itself.

**DON'T FORGET:** Before the night is over take a picture of the group. It sounds cheesy, and I didn't do this myself for the longest time because it felt stupid and ego-centric, but trust me when I say you'll regret it if you don't. You can use these photos for social proof, to post on social media sites and to tag your guests, or as part of a follow up email.

# Post Dinner

O nce the dinner is done it's a pretty awesome feeling. Depending on the group (and how private they are) I will either send an email introduction to them all right after or introduce them all privately on a Facebook message. I'll thank them for investing their time, and will often include one or two points from the dinner in the email, like "I loved John's advice around…" or "I really resonated with…". I also carry a small notebook during dinners for notes. If someone brings up a website name or article in the course of conversation I'll follow up with a resource list in that group email.

After your dinner you can generally expect one or two people to reach out and ask "How can I deliver value to you?"

I used to say "Don't worry about it" or "If I think of something I'll let you know," but now I always ask them if they could connect me with one other really interesting person. Amazing people know other amazing people, so introductions like these can be huge when building your network or trying to find guests for future Mastermind Dinners.

# DOUBLE OPT-IN INTRODUCTIONS

After a dinner you will probably facilitate a few email introductions.
Again, a connector is primed to see connections and to leverage his or
her network to solve problems for others. People fail miserably at introductions when they don't reach out to both parties individually to see
if there is mutual interest in being connected. The connector has to do
the heavy lifting by giving context as to why you're introducing the two
people in the first place.

One of my biggest pet peeves is getting something in my inbox saying
something along the lines of : "Jayson, meet David. I think you two
should know each other."

An unexpected introduction like this puts me in a tough spot as it forces
me to add yet another thing to my to-do list. I'm often so swamped that
I don't have time to reply to the email itself, much less set up a call
to meet someone new. Also, by giving no context whatsoever for the
introduction, it puts the onus on those being introduced to find out the
purpose of the introduction.

Many people are lazy when it comes to introductions and when you do
them poorly it creates unneeded tension, makes you look bad, and can
really burn through your social capital.

You need to be the gatekeeper of your network. I am VERY protective of my relationships and very respectful of people's time. Because of my associations I am asked on a daily basis for introductions. Before I go through step one and get both parties to agree to the introduction I make sure there's a strong and compelling reason as to why I'm doing the introduction in the first place. I've learned to ask "What is your desired outcome with the connection?" This question stops half of those who reach out to me dead in their tracks and forces them to get really clear about what they want or need. You wouldn't believe how many people request a connection to somebody else with virtually no clarity as to what they want out of it. Although a lot of this behind the scenes work is never seen, getting both parties to opt in and setting strong context ensures that every introduction you make has been well vetted.

# FOR BROWNIE POINTS

A nice touch is to loop back to the group a year later and email everyone again saying "Happy anniversary!" or "It's been one year!" as a follow up to check in on everyone and see if you can spark conversation. Be sure to include the picture you took.

# GET CREATIVE!

You now know the ins and outs of running a Mastermind Dinner! Now get creative! This framework can be applied in various ways. The obvious ones are breakfasts and lunches. These are more cost effective to hold than dinners and can work better for some people schedule-wise. But every once in awhile, go beyond a meal meet-up. Become a world class facilitator of experience.

I recently held an axe throwing event for entrepreneurs and it was fantastic. An experience like this takes bonding to a new level because it puts everyone on a level playing field. What I mean by this is that you can have a gathering where someone (because of their level of success) is put on a bit of a pedestal. Getting people to do something outside their comfort zone, something they're not particularly good at, is a recipe for a great bonding experience. Other out of the box experiences could be a behind the scenes tour of a local business, a cooking class or even skydiving. The possibilities are endless.

# FREE RESOURCES

*I didn't write this book for friends, fame, or financial reasons. I wrote it because I am living proof that your network is your net worth. To me, there is no better way to forge a strong network than to host Mastermind Dinners.*

Statistics show that 90% of people don't read past the first chapter of a book. Congratulations, you're in the top 10%! Don't let this new knowledge go to waste. There are seven days in a week and someday isn't one of them. I want you to start planning your first Mastermind Dinner right away. Don't get overwhelmed by the information I've given you here - start small. It's better to take imperfect action than no action at all.

# Need a little incentive?

Take a picture of your dinner and post it to Twitter, Facebook or Instagram (or all three to increase your chances) using the hashtag #Mdinners. Doing so will enter you in a quarterly draw for a $100 Amazon gift card.

As a special bonus to the book I've created a resource page for you which has awesome things like a dinner checklist, 50 networking ice breaker questions, how to do video emails and much more.

- **To access** the resource page visit MastermindDinners.com

- **Have a question?** Join our community! MMTCommunity.com

- **It's free,** and there are some fantastic people in the group to connect with. If you require something more direct I am available for calls on Clarity.fm in support of Pencils of Promise - https://clarity.fm/jaysongaignard

"IF I HAVE SEEN FURTHER
IT IS BY STANDING ON
THE SHOULDERS OF
GIANTS."

~ISAAC NEWTON

# ACKNOWLEDGEMENTS

—∞∞—

M y 29 years on this planet has been comprised of many zigs and zags. Going through the list of people who've had a huge impact on my life would take many pages (and I would be adding new people to the list by the day). In the context of Mastermind Dinners, I have a few friends who've seen similar value in connecting like minded individuals over meals and each of them have had some form of influence on the dinners that I hold. People like Brian Kurtz, Michael Fishman, Ramit Sethi, and Dan Martell.

In fact, if it wasn't for Dan's little "push," I would have never taken the time to write this book.

I want to say a special thank you to all of those who've supported MastermindTalks. Being able to serve an incredible group of leaders and influencers has brought my life a level of depth and fulfillment that is unmatched.

Thank you to all my beta readers from the MMTcommunity who gave me such incredible feedback on the book before launching: Kenton Ho, Derek Coburn, Rikke Hansen, Steve Sisler, Jason Koprowski, Harry Duran, Radiris Diaz, Nick DiNardo, Billy Murphy, James Tonn, Julia

Wojnar, Janel DuRoss, Diana Goodwin, Sean Gleeson, Chandra Clarke, Sara Stibitz, Tamas Perlaky, Louise Hendon, Paul Collins, Joshua Jordison, Jonathan Goodman, Laura Tinti, Sharon Dubois, Luke Harvard, Brad Mills, Patrick Vlaskovits. Many of your well thought out suggestions will be found in our expanded version of the book.

Mentors have always been crucial to my success. I currently have two in my life who I owe the majority of my current success (and sanity) to. Kourosh Assef and Jay Georgi, you both hold me to a higher standard than I hold myself and I can never properly express how much your mentorship and guidance means to me.

Before closing off, I want to acknowledge my lovely wife Kandis. There's a saying that a man's loyalty is tested when he has everything and a woman's loyalty is tested when her man has nothing. My wife stood by me when we were going through the thick of things, and I'll never forget that.

I'm a firm believer that you should judge a man by the radiance of his woman, and I am committed to keep her lit up as long as I can.

Just as a side note, my wife did the editing for this project, so if you felt like the book was structured in a clear and actionable way, it's because of her work. She does take on other editing projects from time to time so don't hesitate to reach her at Kandis@mastermindtalks.com if you're interested in her services.

# MASTERMIND DINNERS

*by*

## JAYSON GAIGNARD

VERSION 1.0

TO STAY UP TO DATE WITH NEW VERSIONS,
AND GET ACCESS TO FREE BOOK RESOURCES,
VISIT MASTERMINDDINNERS.COM

MANUSCRIPT FORMATTED BY: ERIN TYLER
ISBN: 9780692360026

Made in the USA
San Bernardino, CA
20 March 2015